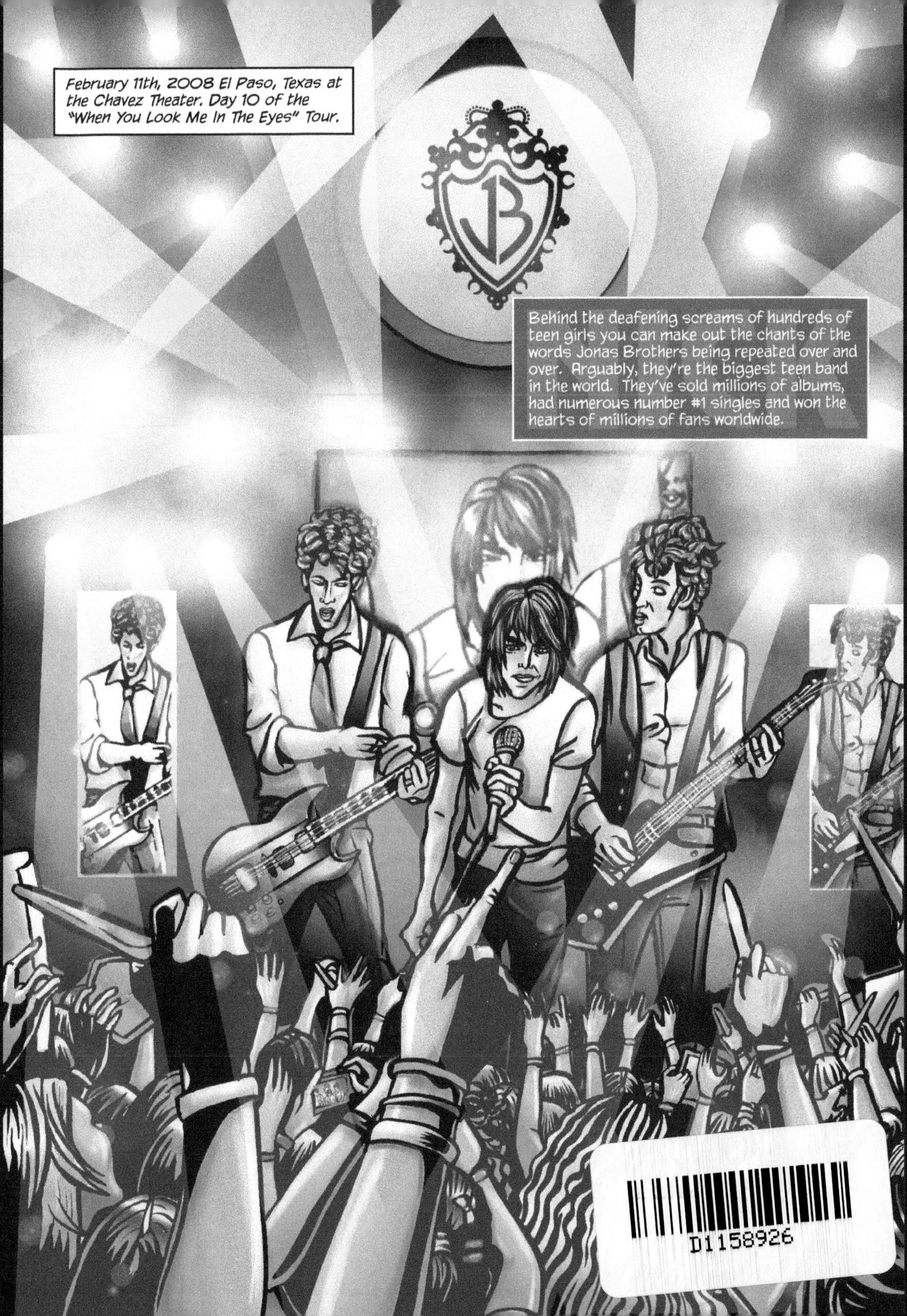
February 11th, 2008 El Paso, Texas at the Chavez Theater. Day 10 of the "When You Look Me In The Eyes" Tour.
Behind the deafening screams of hundreds of teen girls you can make out the chants of the words Jonas Brothers being repeated over and over. Arguably, they're the biggest teen band in the world. They've sold millions of albums, had numerous number #1 singles and won the hearts of millions of fans worldwide.

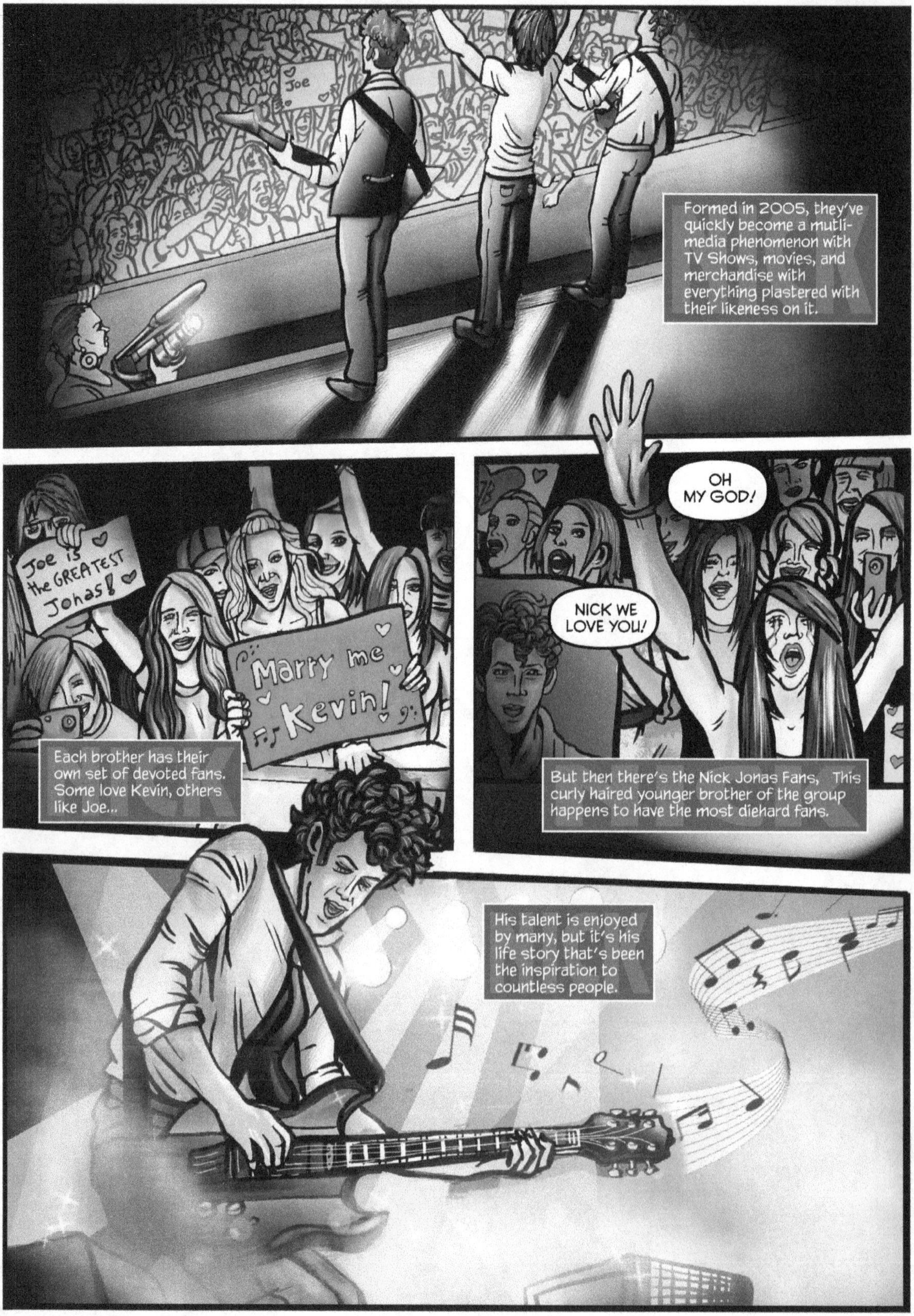
Joe
Formed in 2005, they've quickly become a mutli-media phenomenon with TV Shows, movies, and merchandise with everything plastered with their likeness on it.
Joe is the GREATEST Jonas!
Marry me Kevin!
Each brother has their own set of devoted fans. Some love Kevin, others like Joe...
OH MY GOD!
NICK WE LOVE YOU!
But then there's the Nick Jonas Fans, This curly haired younger brother of the group happens to have the most diehard fans.
His talent is enjoyed by many, but it's his life story that's been the inspiration to countless people.

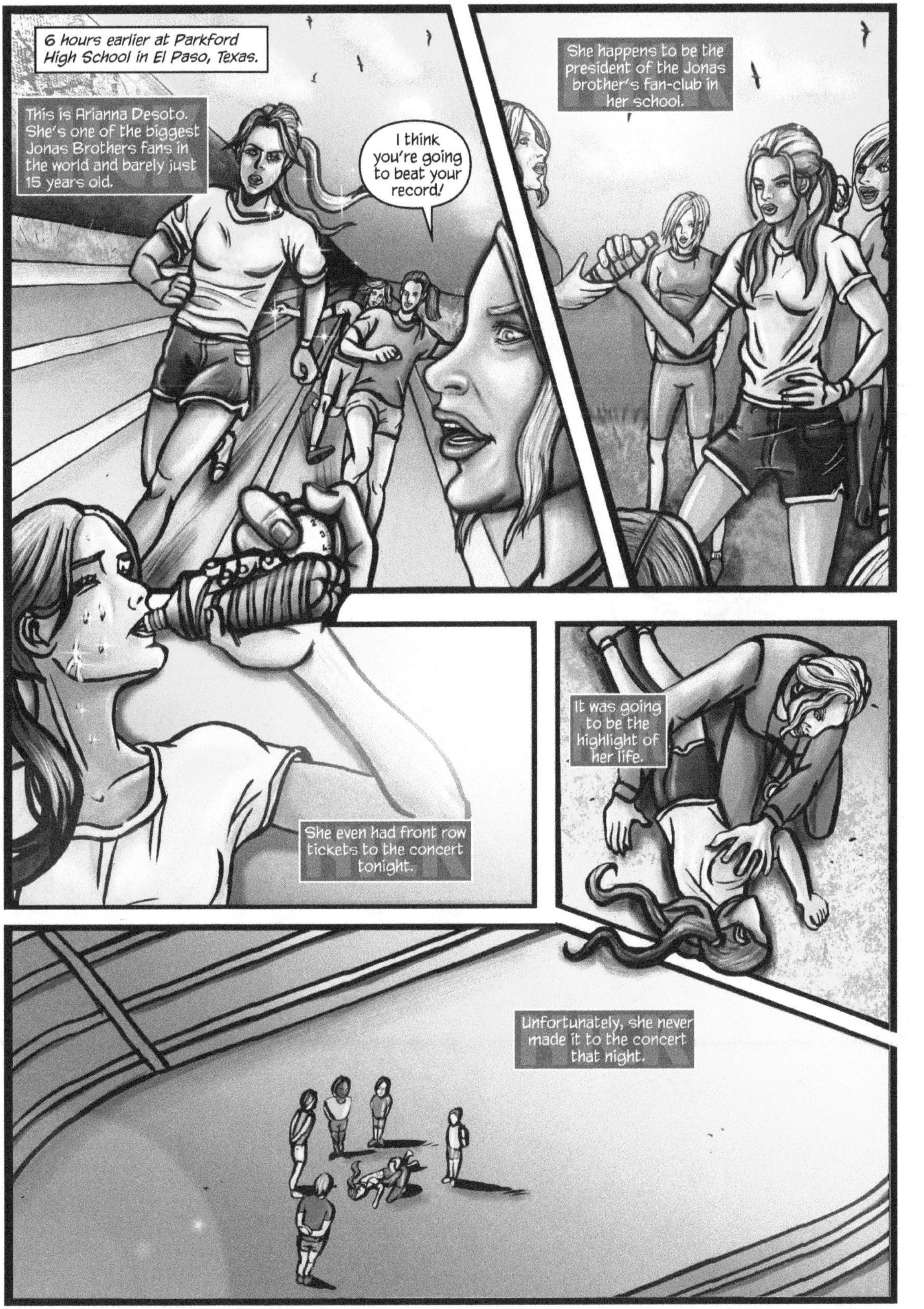
6 hours earlier at Parkford High School in El Paso, Texas.
This is Arianna Desoto. She's one of the biggest Jonas Brothers fans in the world and barely just 15 years old.
I think you're going to beat your record!
She happens to be the president of the Jonas brother's fan-club in her school.
She even had front row tickets to the concert tonight.
It was going to be the highlight of her life.
Unfortunately, she never made it to the concert that night.

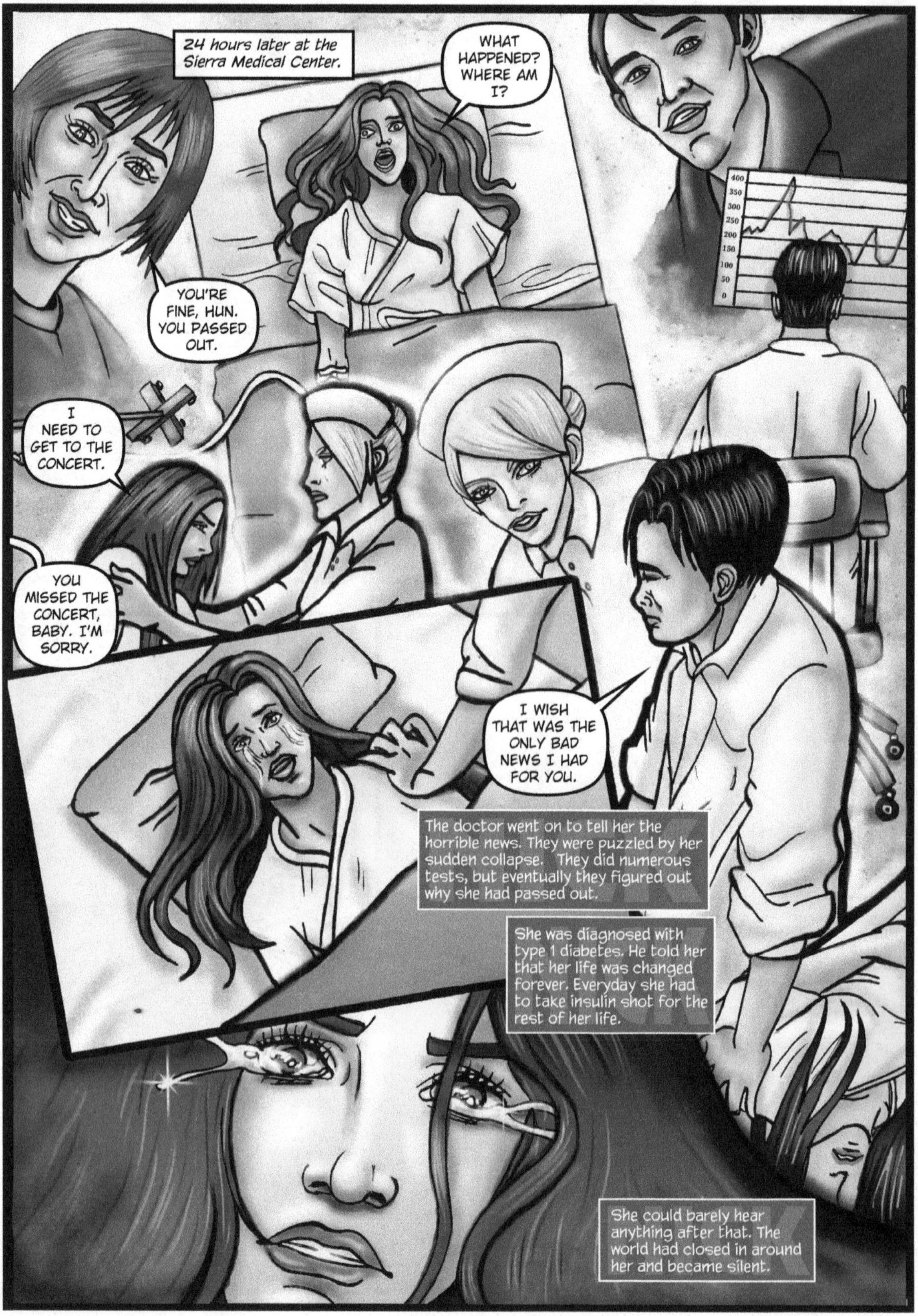
24 hours later at the Sierra Medical Center.
WHAT HAPPENED? WHERE AM I?
YOU'RE FINE, HUN. YOU PASSED OUT.
I NEED TO GET TO THE CONCERT.
YOU MISSED THE CONCERT, BABY. I'M SORRY.
I WISH THAT WAS THE ONLY BAD NEWS I HAD FOR YOU.
The doctor went on to tell her the horrible news. They were puzzled by her sudden collapse. They did numerous tests, but eventually they figured out why she had passed out.
She was diagnosed with type 1 diabetes. He told her that her life was changed forever. Everyday she had to take insulin shot for the rest of her life.
She could barely hear anything after that. The world had closed in around her and became silent.

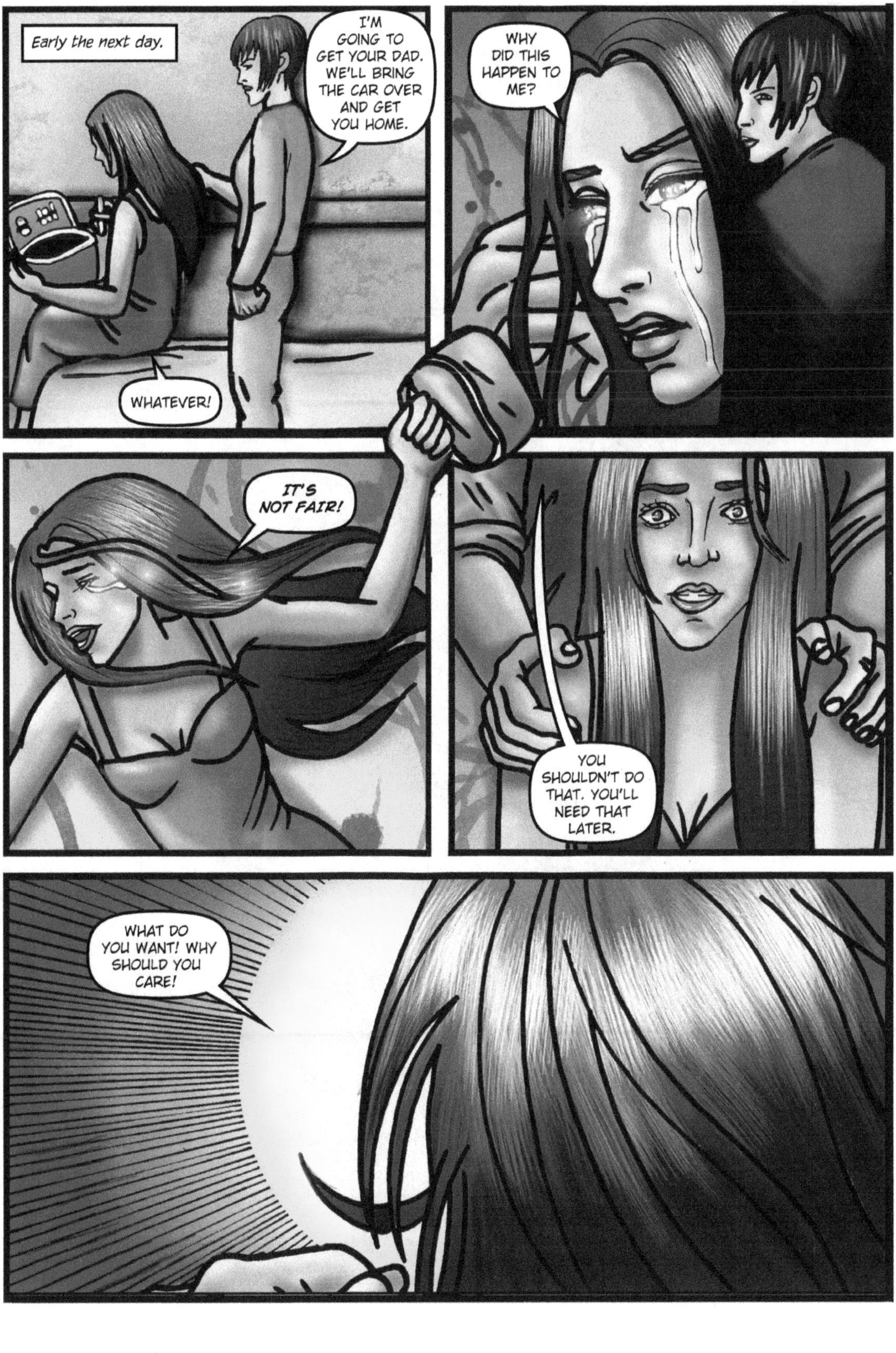
Early the next day.
I'M GOING TO GET YOUR DAD. WE'LL BRING THE CAR OVER AND GET YOU HOME.
WHATEVER!
WHY DID THIS HAPPEN TO ME?
IT'S NOT FAIR!
YOU SHOULDN'T DO THAT. YOU'LL NEED THAT LATER.
WHAT DO YOU WANT! WHY SHOULD YOU CARE!

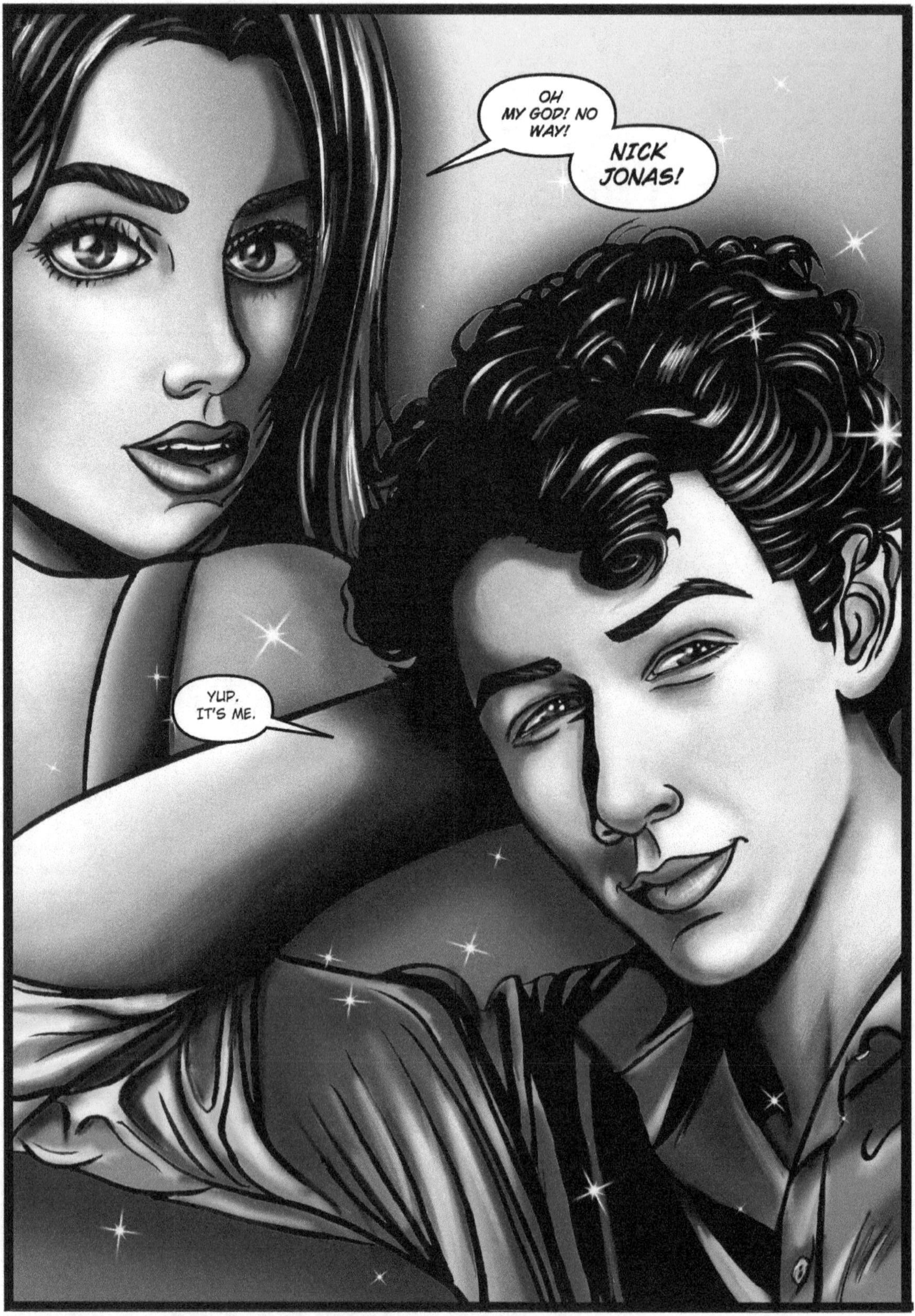
OH MY GOD! NO WAY!
NICK JONAS!
YUP, IT'S ME.

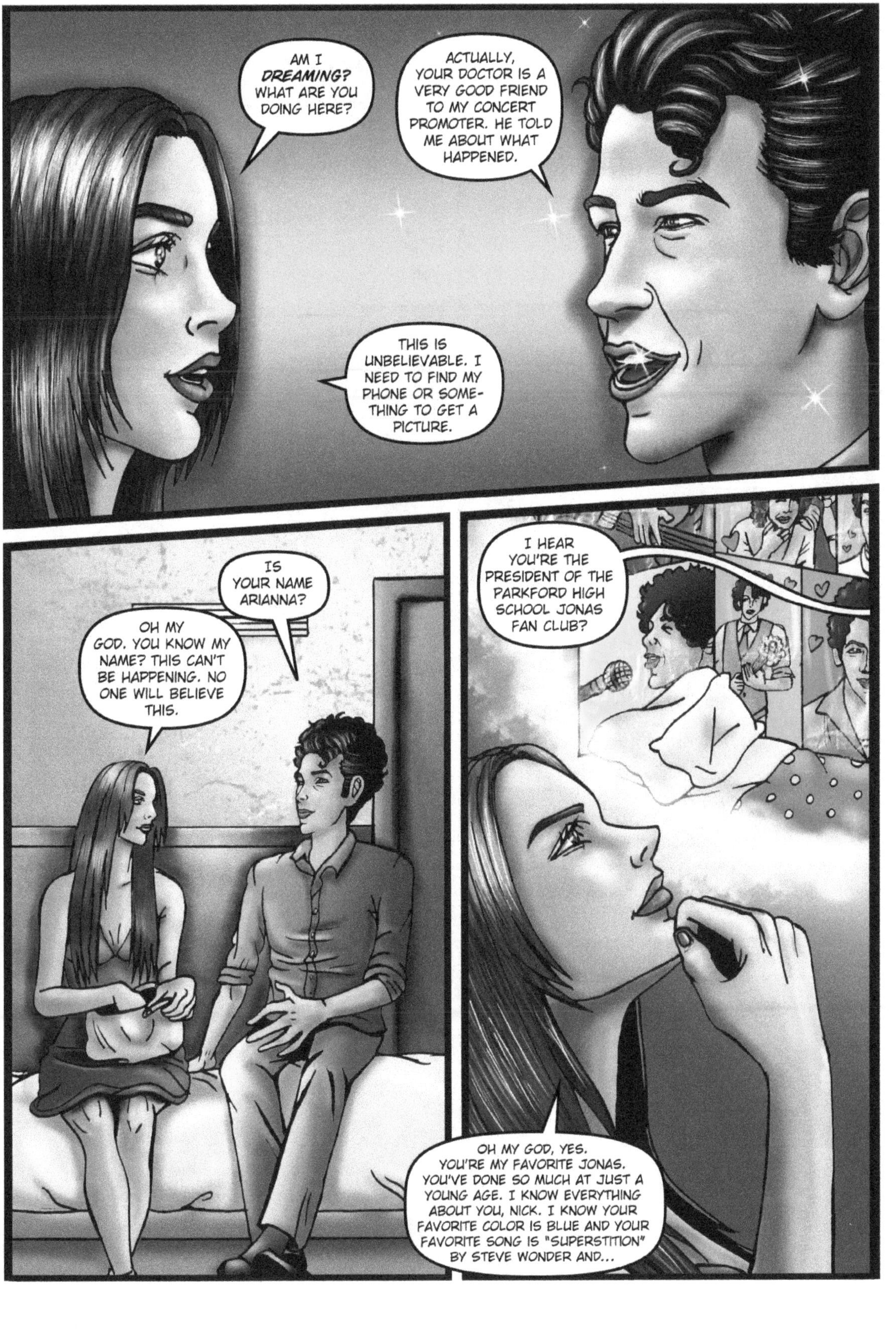
AM I *DREAMING?* WHAT ARE YOU DOING HERE?
ACTUALLY, YOUR DOCTOR IS A VERY GOOD FRIEND TO MY CONCERT PROMOTER. HE TOLD ME ABOUT WHAT HAPPENED.
THIS IS UNBELIEVABLE. I NEED TO FIND MY PHONE OR SOME-THING TO GET A PICTURE.
IS YOUR NAME ARIANNA?
OH MY GOD. YOU KNOW MY NAME? THIS CAN'T BE HAPPENING. NO ONE WILL BELIEVE THIS.
I HEAR YOU'RE THE PRESIDENT OF THE PARKFORD HIGH SCHOOL JONAS FAN CLUB?
OH MY GOD, YES. YOU'RE MY FAVORITE JONAS. YOU'VE DONE SO MUCH AT JUST A YOUNG AGE. I KNOW EVERYTHING ABOUT YOU, NICK. I KNOW YOUR FAVORITE COLOR IS BLUE AND YOUR FAVORITE SONG IS "SUPERSTITION" BY STEVE WONDER AND...

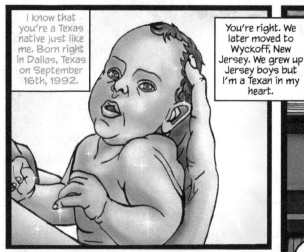

I know that you're a Texas native just like me. Born right in Dallas, Texas on September 16th, 1992.

You're right. We later moved to Wyckoff, New Jersey. We grew up Jersey boys but I'm a Texan in my heart.

NICHOLAS, PLEASE GET DOWN FROM THERE.

NO, MAMA. I NEED PRACTICE. I'M GONNA BE ON BROADWAY.

Both of my parents were musicians so I guess you can say show business was in my blood and I always knew what I wanted to do in life.

BABY, BYE, BYE, BYE...

Me and my brothers used to put on little stage shows in the basement and we used to charge people 5 bucks to see us.

We also self taught ourselves to play the guitar. Even to this day I can't read a sheet of music, but I can definitely rock out. It was much more fun for us than it was for my mom.

That is amazing.

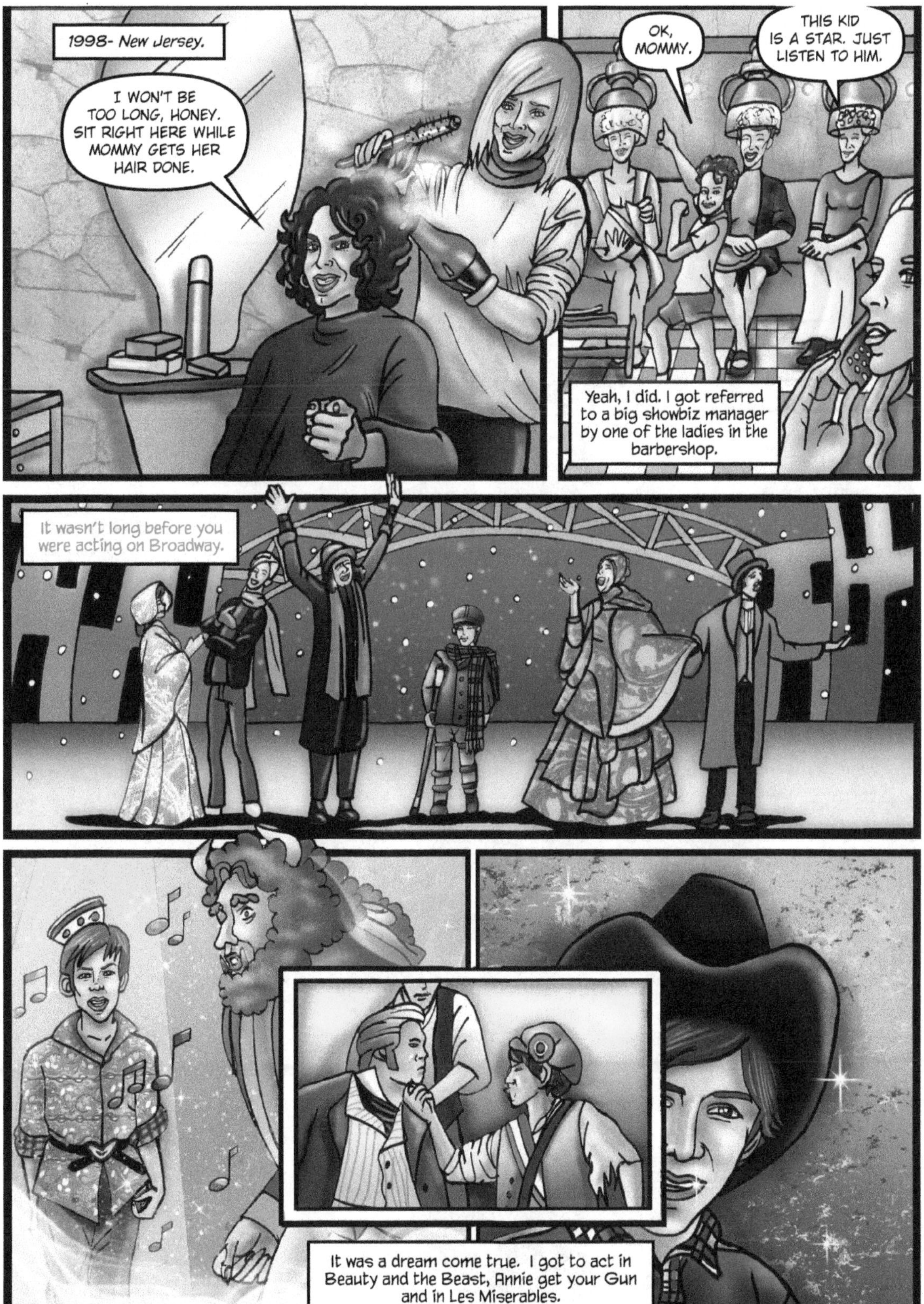
1998- New Jersey.
I WON'T BE TOO LONG, HONEY. SIT RIGHT HERE WHILE MOMMY GETS HER HAIR DONE.
OK, MOMMY.
THIS KID IS A STAR. JUST LISTEN TO HIM.
Yeah, I did. I got referred to a big showbiz manager by one of the ladies in the barbershop.
It wasn't long before you were acting on Broadway.
It was a dream come true. I got to act in Beauty and the Beast, Annie get your Gun and in Les Miserables.

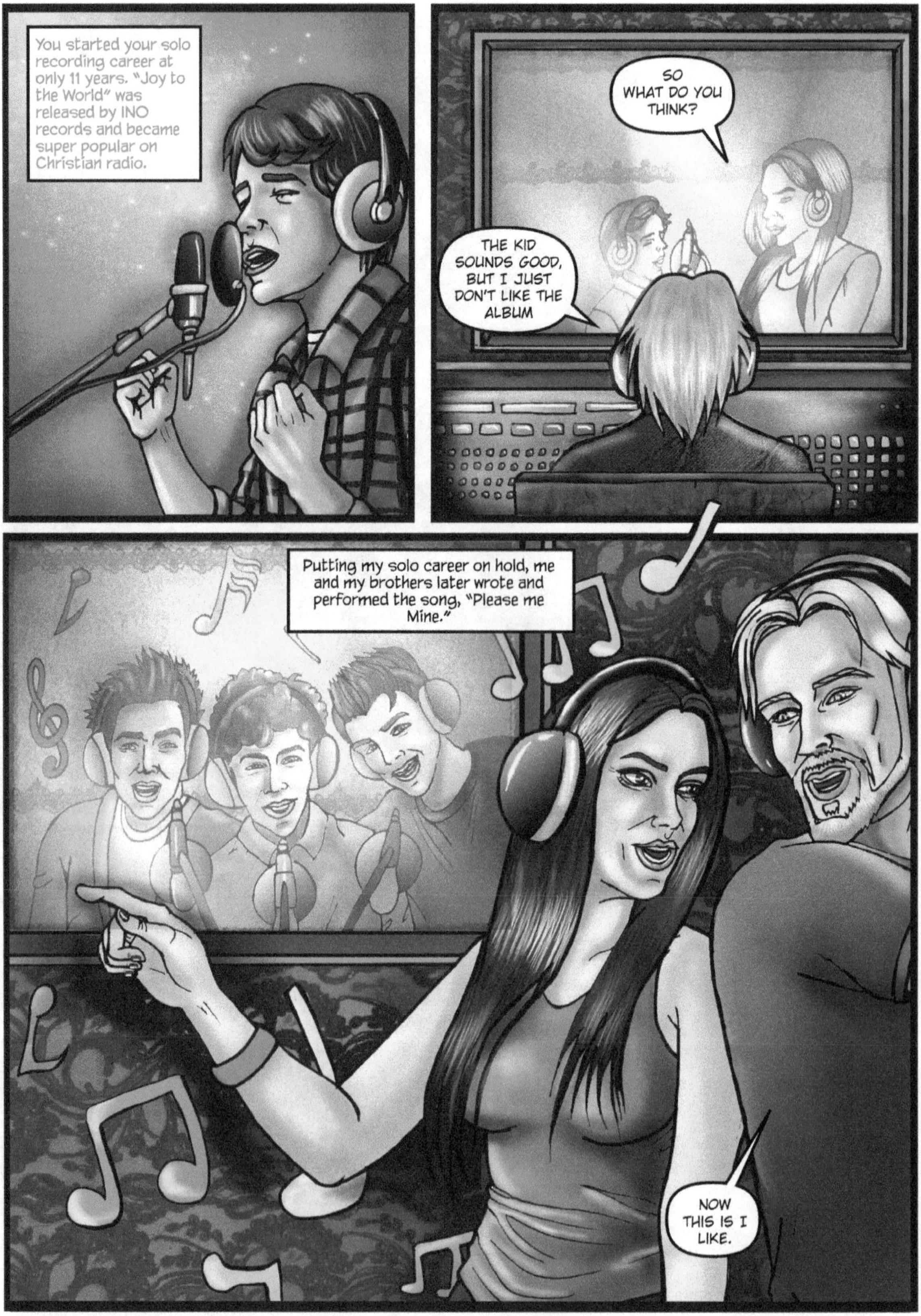
You started your solo recording career at only 11 years. "Joy to the World" was released by INO records and became super popular on Christian radio.
SO WHAT DO YOU THINK?
THE KID SOUNDS GOOD, BUT I JUST DON'T LIKE THE ALBUM
Putting my solo career on hold, me and my brothers later wrote and performed the song, "Please me Mine."
NOW THIS IS I LIKE.

Before we even know it, we were signed to Colombia Records and the Jonas Brothers band was born. Our first album "It's about time" got released and we started our first concert tour.

Emotional success was only short term though. We soon saw the reality of show business.

I'M SORRY GUYS. THE COMPANY WANTS TO LET YOU GO FROM YOUR CONTRACT. SALES ON THE ALBUM WERE NOT WHAT THEIR WANTED.

NO WAY.

THAT SUCKS!

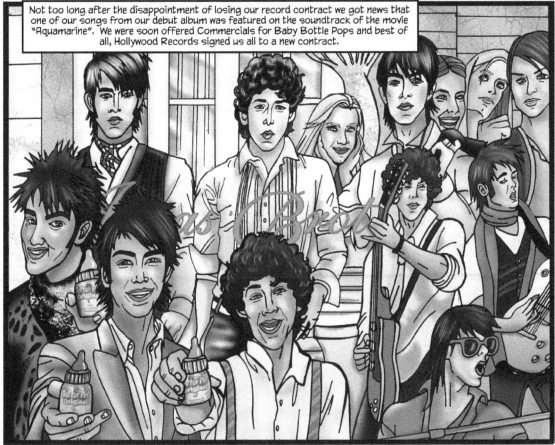

Not too long after the disappointment of losing our record contract we got news that one of our songs from our debut album was featured on the soundtrack of the movie "Aquamarine". We were soon offered Commercials for Baby Bottle Pops and best of all, Hollywood Records signed us all to a new contract.

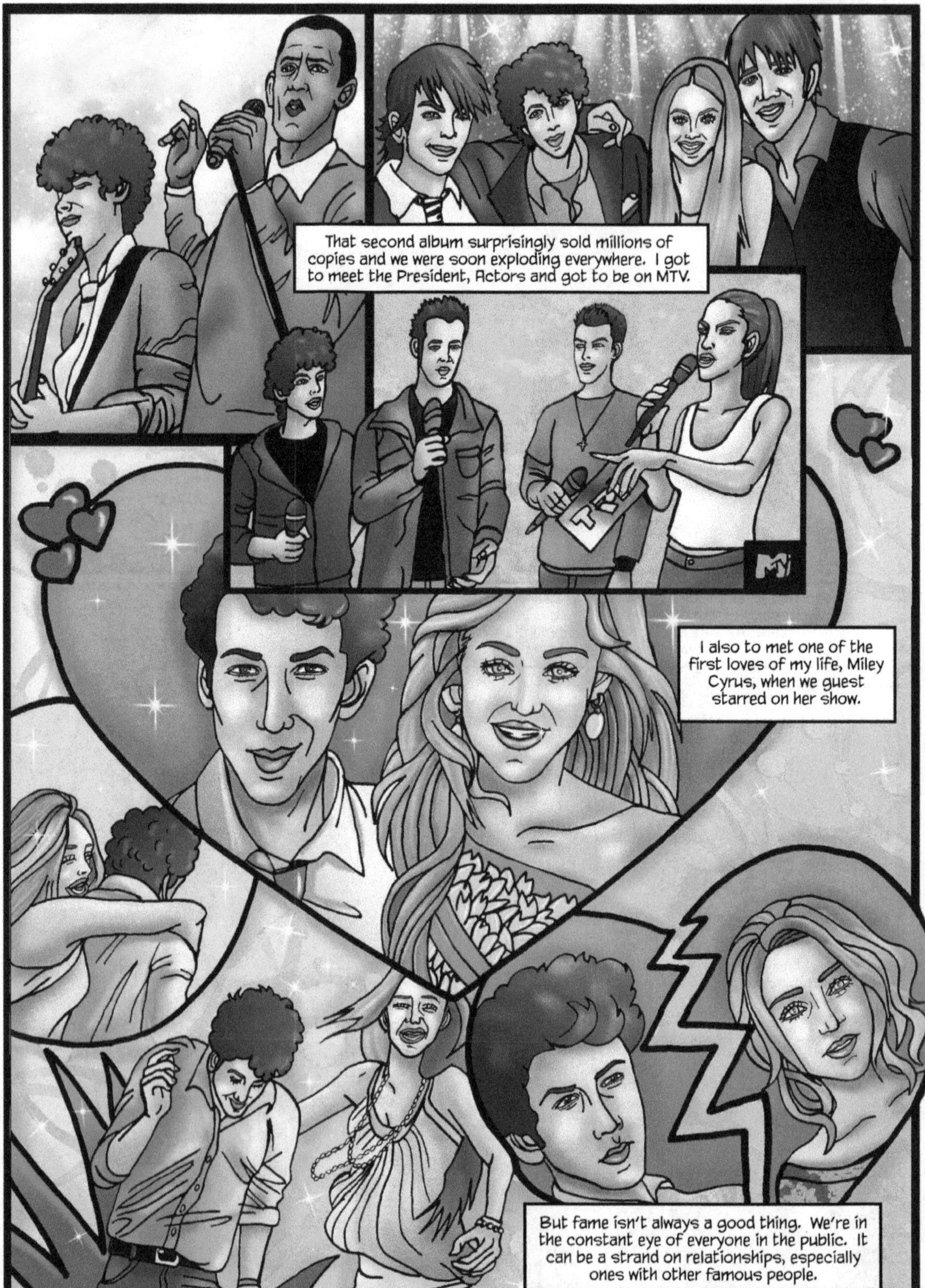
That second album surprisingly sold millions of copies and we were soon exploding everywhere. I got to meet the President, Actors and got to be on MTV.
I also to met one of the first loves of my life, Miley Cyrus, when we guest starred on her show.
But fame isn't always a good thing. We're in the constant eye of everyone in the public. It can be a strand on relationships, especially ones with other famous people.

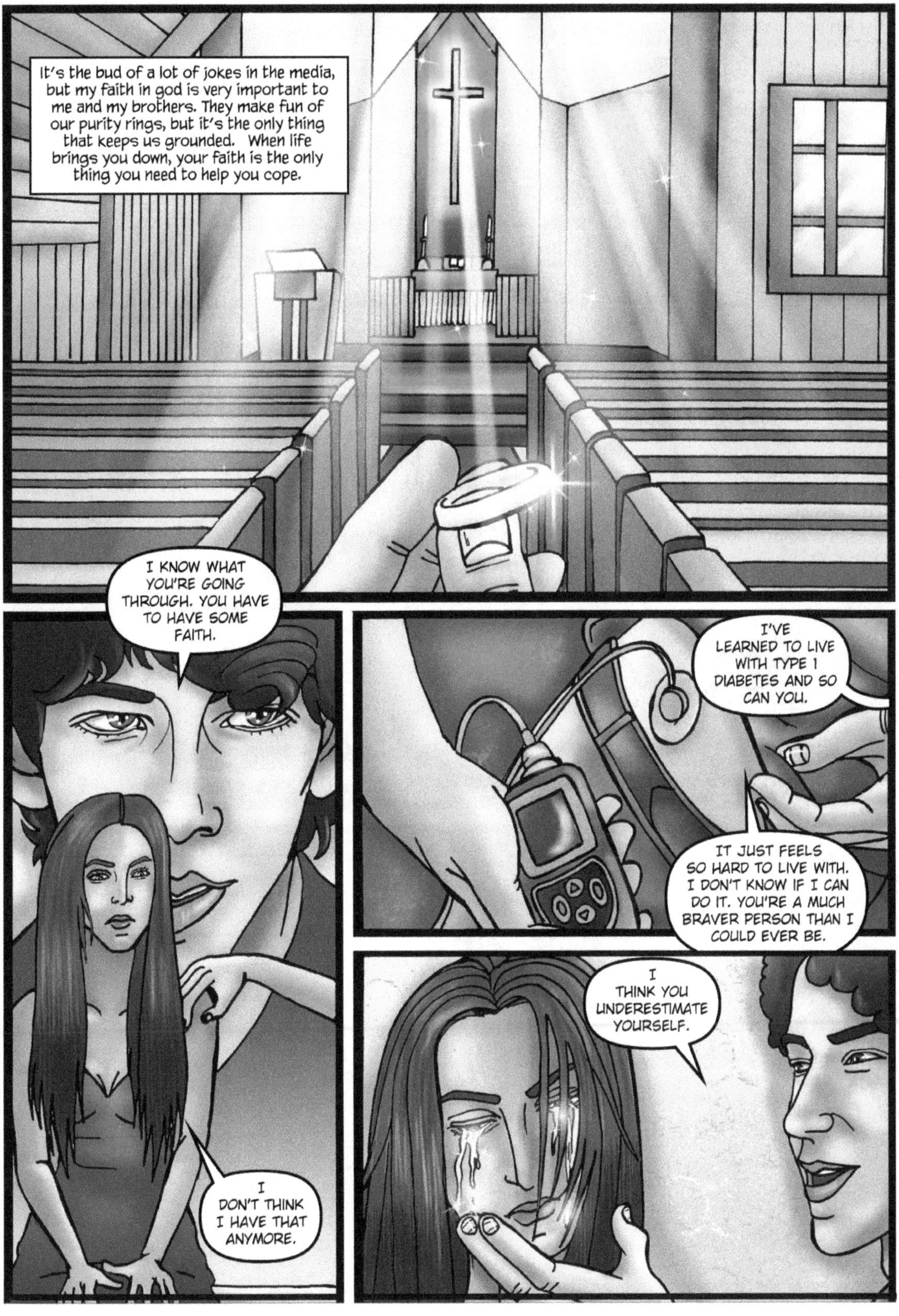
It's the bud of a lot of jokes in the media, but my faith in god is very important to me and my brothers. They make fun of our purity rings, but it's the only thing that keeps us grounded. When life brings you down, your faith is the only thing you need to help you cope.
I KNOW WHAT YOU'RE GOING THROUGH. YOU HAVE TO HAVE SOME FAITH.
I DON'T THINK I HAVE THAT ANYMORE.
I'VE LEARNED TO LIVE WITH TYPE 1 DIABETES AND SO CAN YOU.
IT JUST FEELS SO HARD TO LIVE WITH. I DON'T KNOW IF I CAN DO IT. YOU'RE A MUCH BRAVER PERSON THAN I COULD EVER BE.
I THINK YOU UNDERESTIMATE YOURSELF.

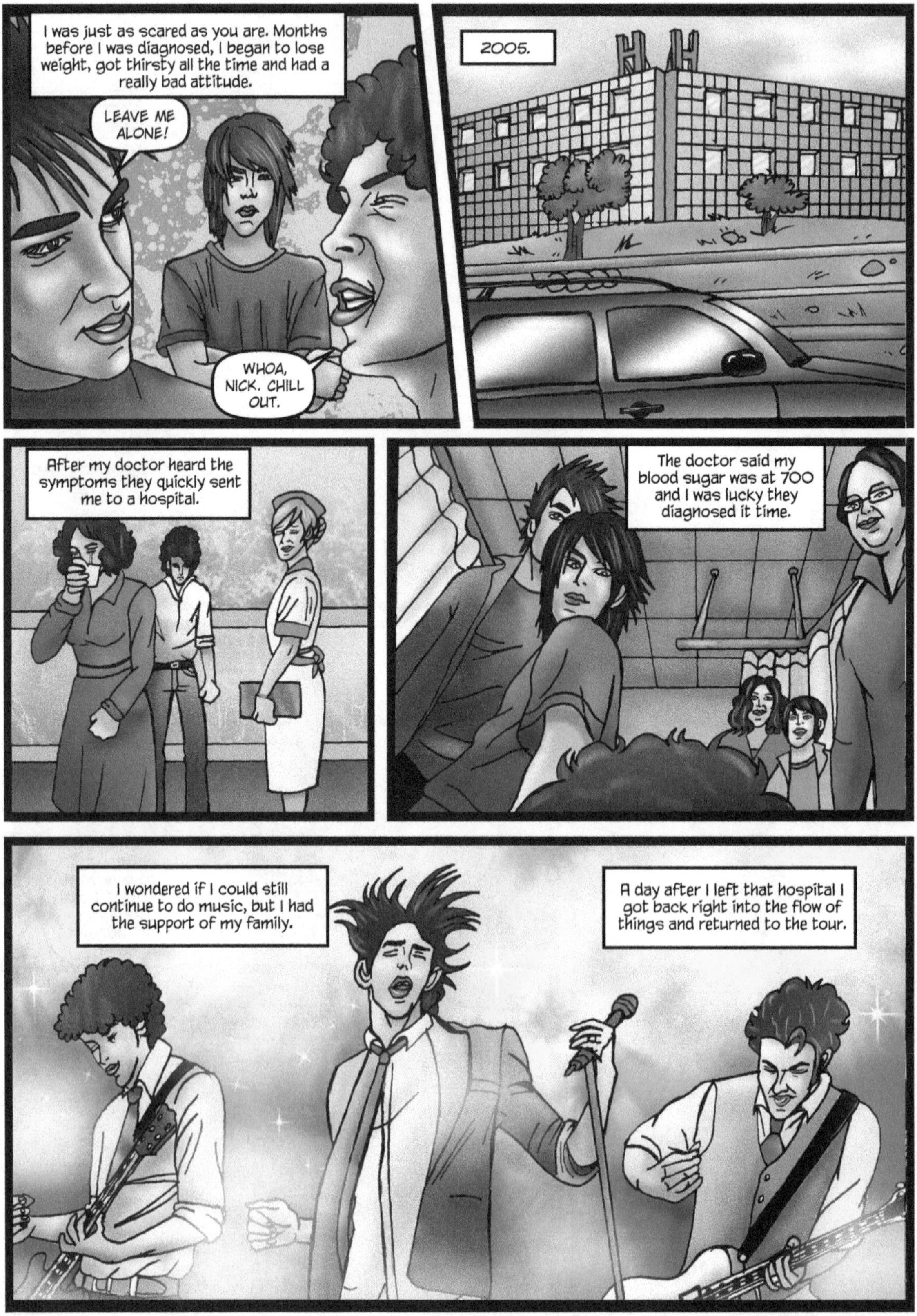
I was just as scared as you are. Months before I was diagnosed, I began to lose weight, got thirsty all the time and had a really bad attitude.
LEAVE ME ALONE!
WHOA, NICK. CHILL OUT.
2005.
After my doctor heard the symptoms they quickly sent me to a hospital.
The doctor said my blood sugar was at 700 and I was lucky they diagnosed it time.
I wondered if I could still continue to do music, but I had the support of my family.
A day after I left that hospital I got back right into the flow of things and returned to the tour.

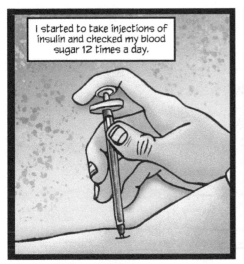

I started to take injections of insulin and checked my blood sugar 12 times a day.

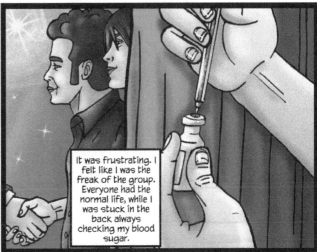

It was frustrating. I felt like I was the freak of the group. Everyone had the normal life, while I was stuck in the back always checking my blood sugar.

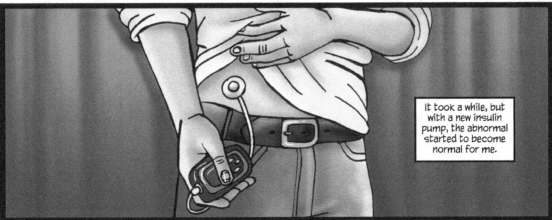

It took a while, but with a new insulin pump, the abnormal started to become normal for me.

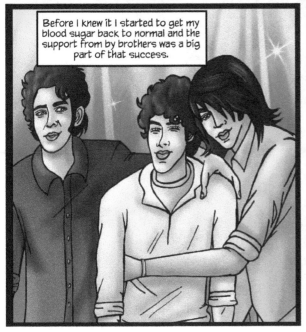

Before I knew it I started to get my blood sugar back to normal and the support from by brothers was a big part of that success.

MY PARENTS DO SEEM VERY SUPPORTIVE OF ME.

IT'S HARD AT FIRST, BUT YOU'LL GET USED TO IT. TRUST ME. I DON'T THINK I COULD HAVE MANAGED IT WITHOUT THE HELP OF MY PARENTS OR FAITH IN GOD.

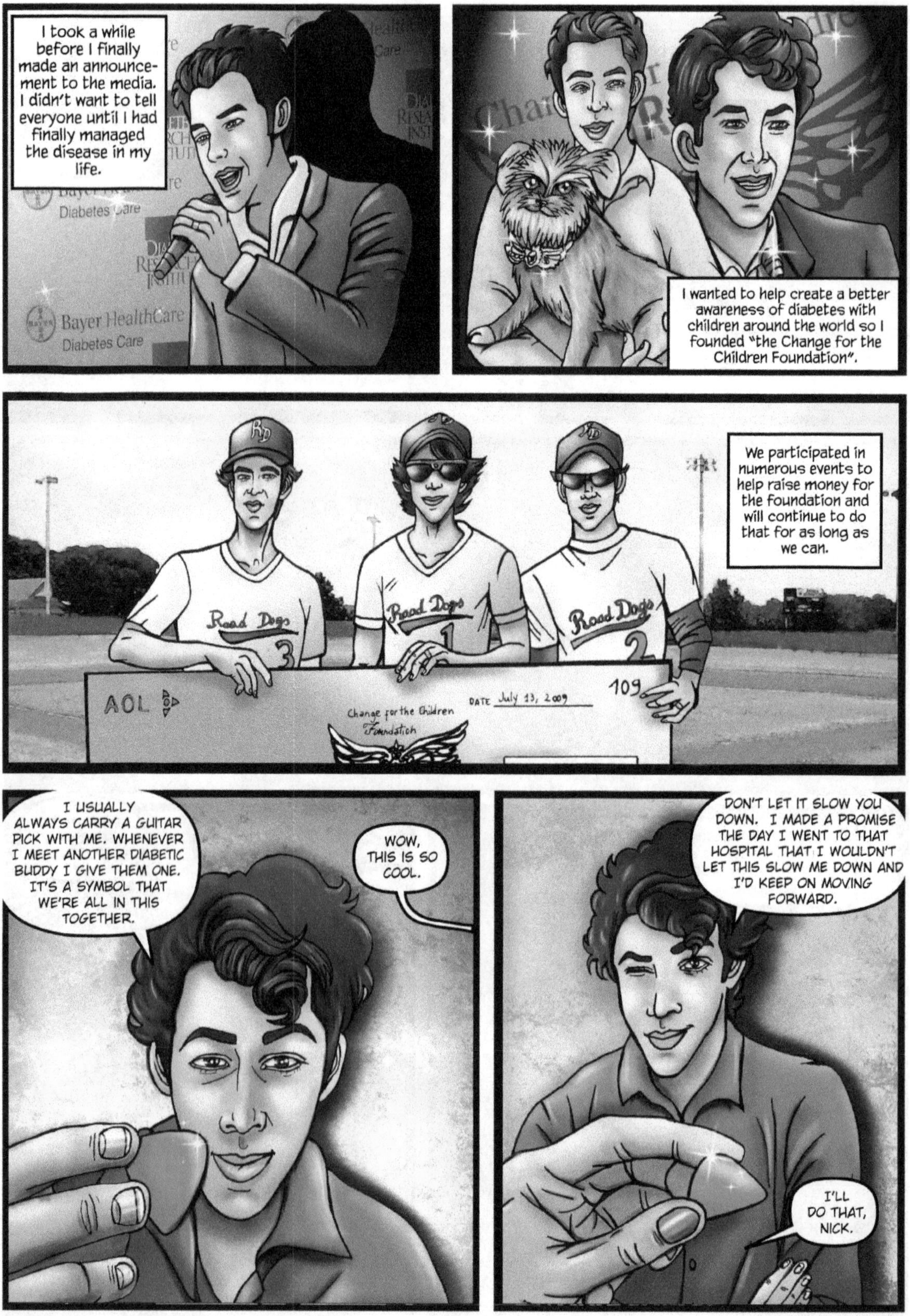
I took a while before I finally made an announcement to the media. I didn't want to tell everyone until I had finally managed the disease in my life.
Bayer HealthCare
Diabetes Care
I wanted to help create a better awareness of diabetes with children around the world so I founded "the Change for the Children Foundation".
We participated in numerous events to help raise money for the foundation and will continue to do that for as long as we can.
Road Dogs 3
Road Dogs 1
Road Dogs 2
AOL
DATE July 13, 2009
109
Change for the Children Foundation
I USUALLY ALWAYS CARRY A GUITAR PICK WITH ME. WHENEVER I MEET ANOTHER DIABETIC BUDDY I GIVE THEM ONE. IT'S A SYMBOL THAT WE'RE ALL IN THIS TOGETHER.
WOW, THIS IS SO COOL.
DON'T LET IT SLOW YOU DOWN. I MADE A PROMISE THE DAY I WENT TO THAT HOSPITAL THAT I WOULDN'T LET THIS SLOW ME DOWN AND I'D KEEP ON MOVING FORWARD.
I'LL DO THAT, NICK.

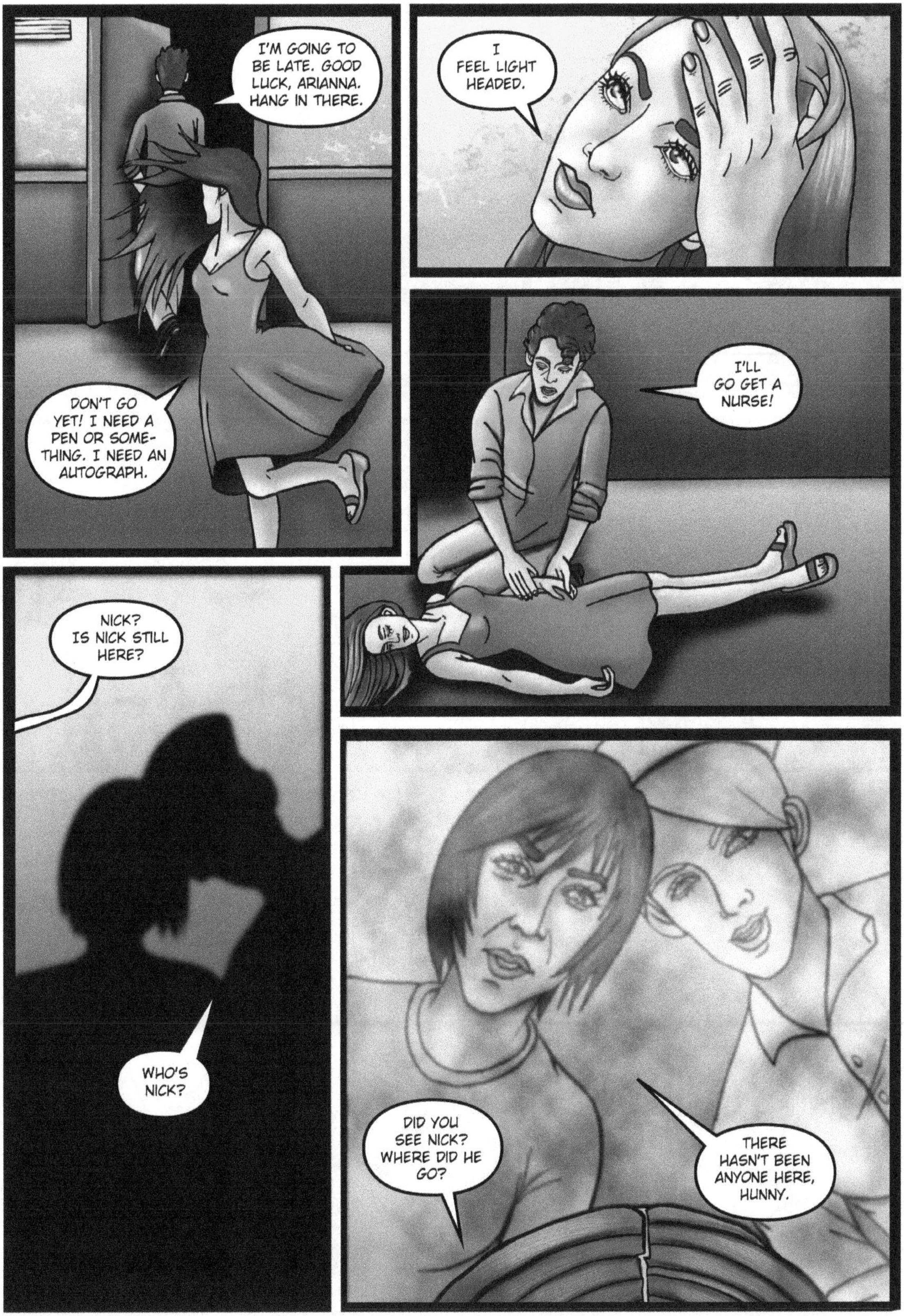
I'M GOING TO BE LATE. GOOD LUCK, ARIANNA. HANG IN THERE.
DON'T GO YET! I NEED A PEN OR SOME-THING. I NEED AN AUTOGRAPH.
I FEEL LIGHT HEADED.
I'LL GO GET A NURSE!
NICK? IS NICK STILL HERE?
WHO'S NICK?
DID YOU SEE NICK? WHERE DID HE GO?
THERE HASN'T BEEN ANYONE HERE, HUNNY.

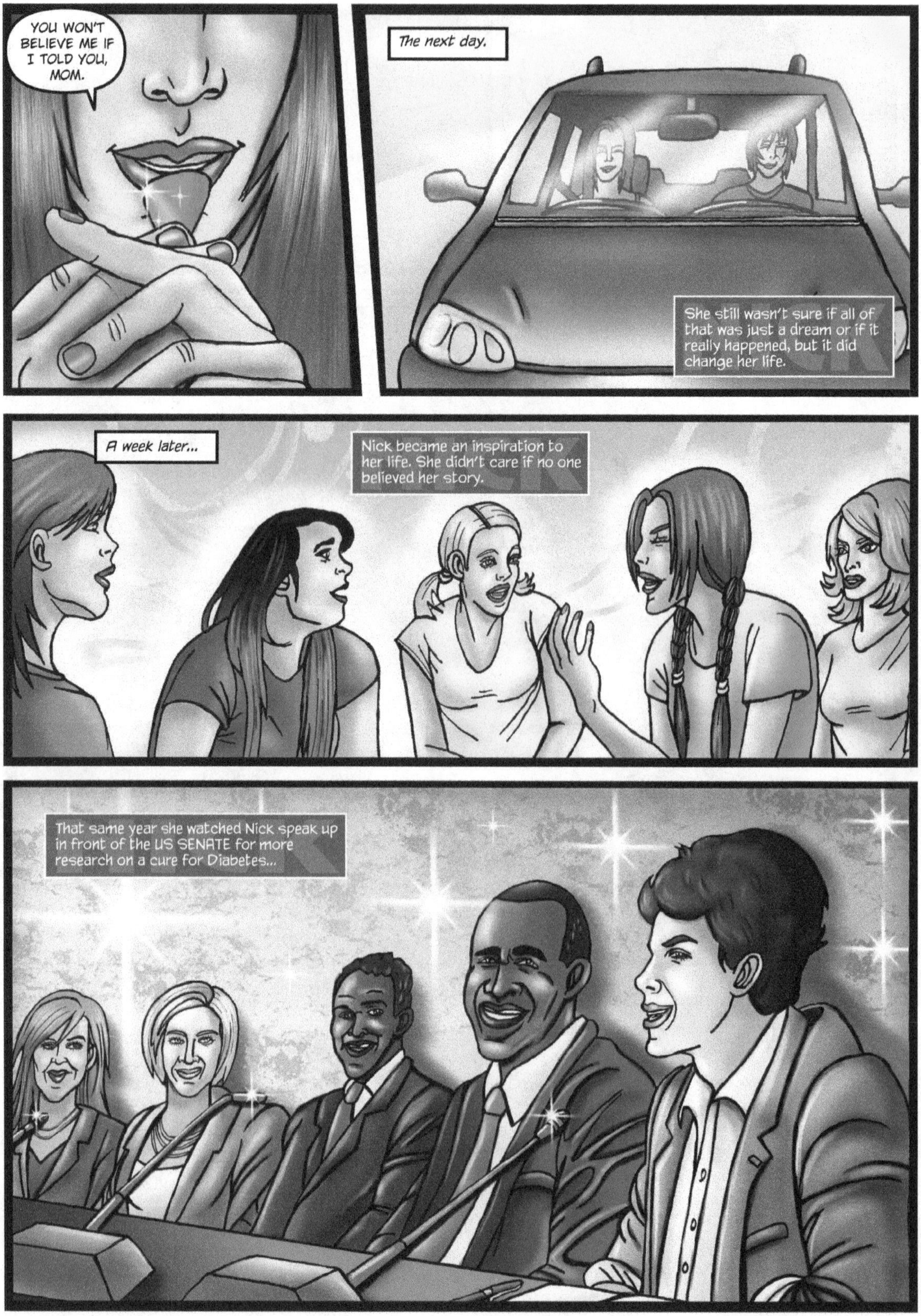
YOU WON'T BELIEVE ME IF I TOLD YOU, MOM.
The next day.
She still wasn't sure if all of that was just a dream or if it really happened, but it did change her life.
A week later...
Nick became an inspiration to her life. She didn't care if no one believed her story.
That same year she watched Nick speak up in front of the US SENATE for more research on a cure for Diabetes...

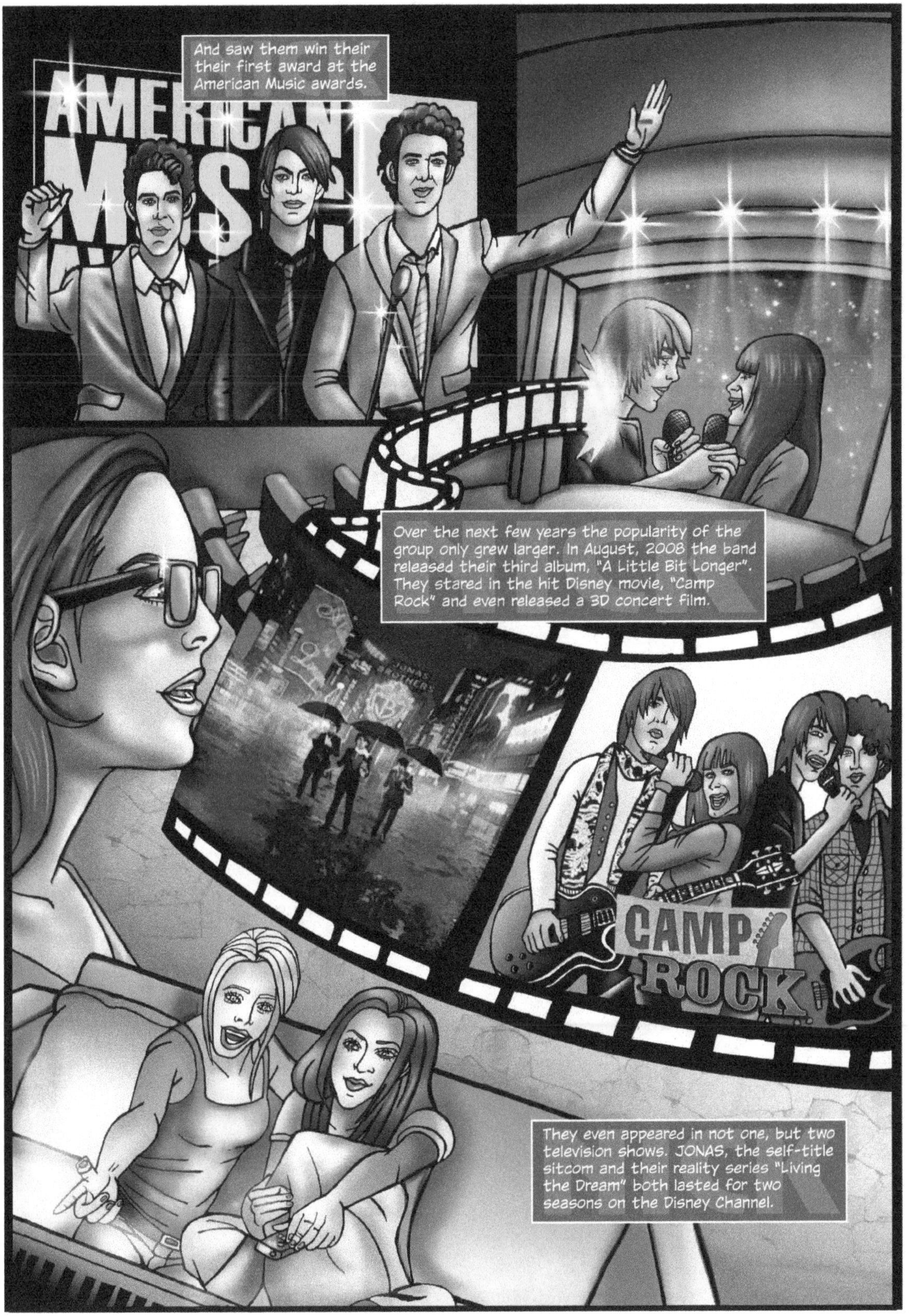
And saw them win their their first award at the American Music awards.
AMERICAN MUS
Over the next few years the popularity of the group only grew larger. In August, 2008 the band released their third album, "A Little Bit Longer". They stared in the hit Disney movie, "Camp Rock" and even released a 3D concert film.
CAMP ROCK
They even appeared in not one, but two television shows. JONAS, the self-title sitcom and their reality series "Living the Dream" both lasted for two seasons on the Disney Channel.

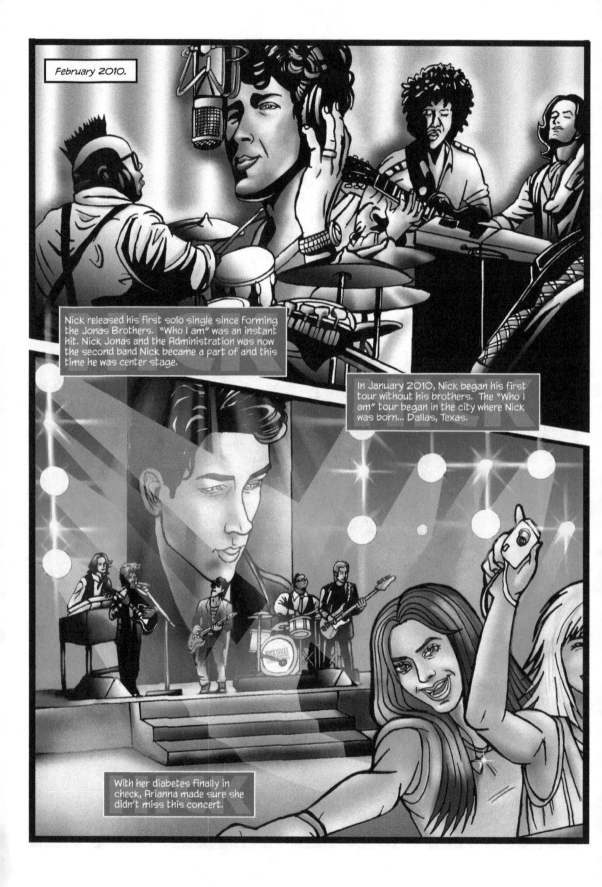

February 2010.

Nick released his first solo single since forming the Jonas Brothers. "Who I am" was an instant hit. Nick Jonas and the Administration was now the second band Nick became a part of and this time he was center stage.

In January 2010, Nick began his first tour without his brothers. The "Who I am" tour began in the city where Nick was born... Dallas, Texas.

With her diabetes finally in check, Arianna made sure she didn't miss this concert.

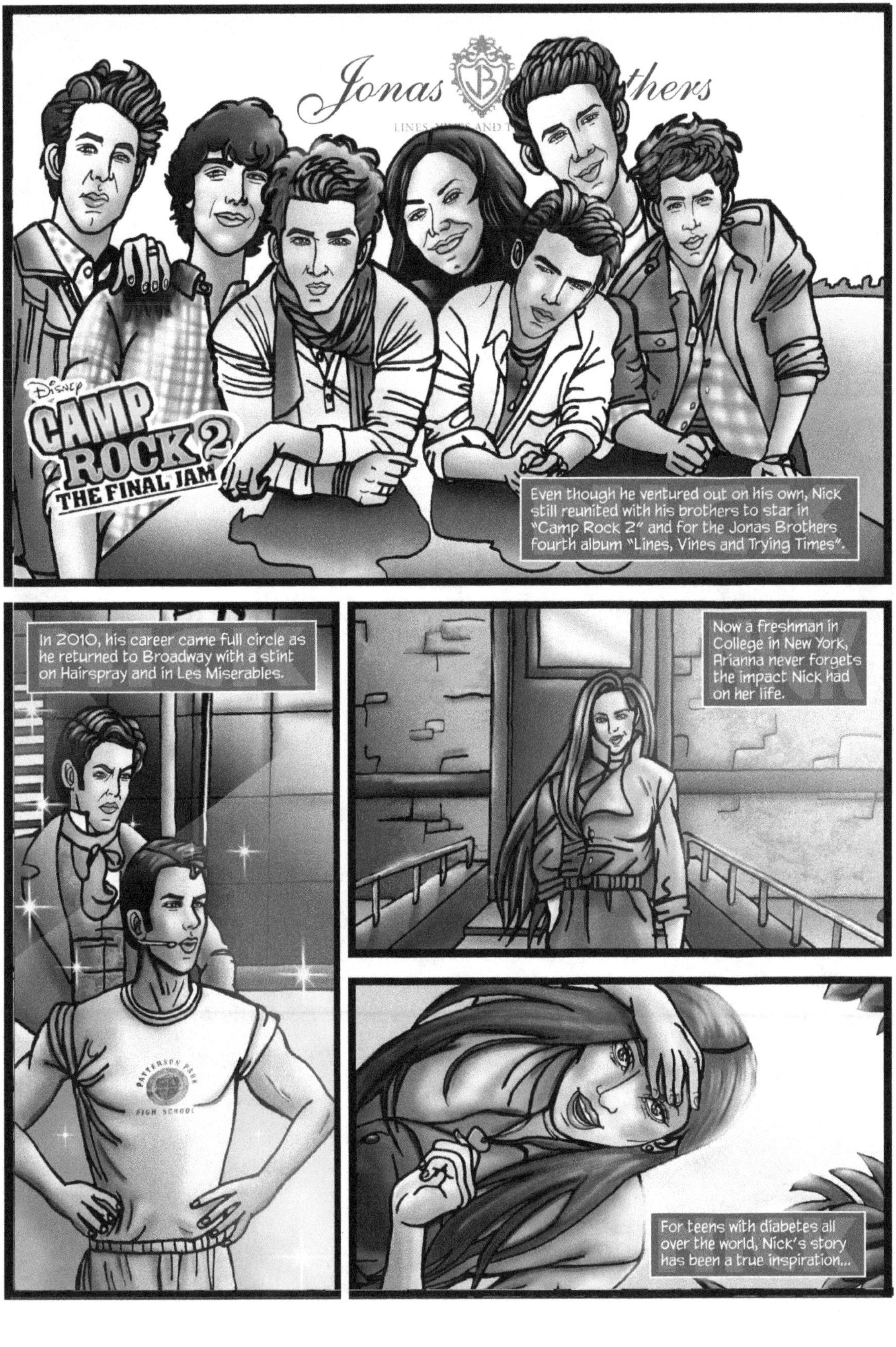
Jonas
Disney
CAMP ROCK 2
THE FINAL JAM
Even though he ventured out on his own, Nick still reunited with his brothers to star in "Camp Rock 2" and for the Jonas Brothers fourth album "Lines, Vines and Trying Times".
In 2010, his career came full circle as he returned to Broadway with a stint on Hairspray and in Les Miserables.
Now a freshman in College in New York, Arianna never forgets the impact Nick had on her life.
For teens with diabetes all over the world, Nick's story has been a true inspiration...

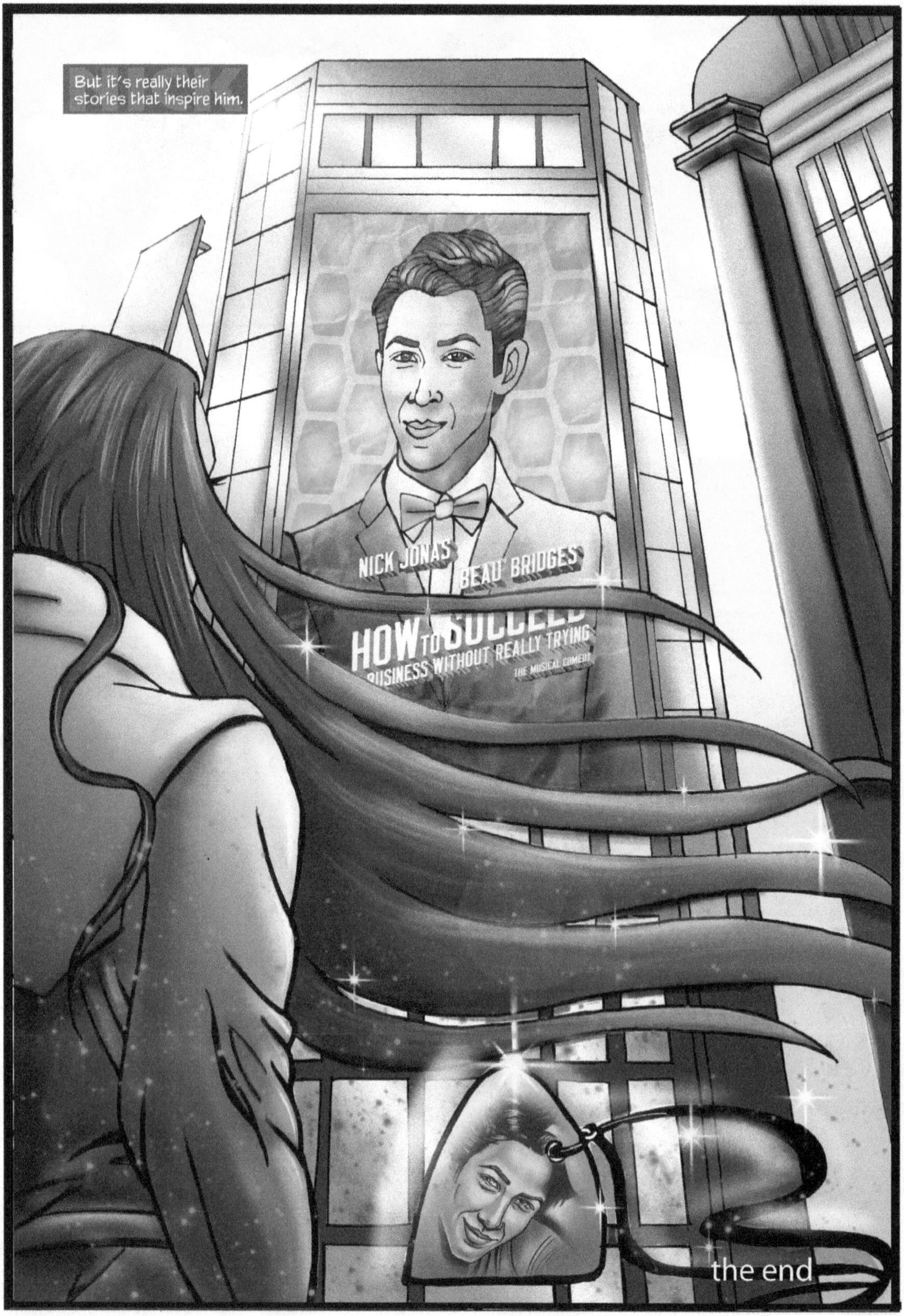
But it's really their stories that inspire him.
NICK JONAS
BEAU BRIDGES
THE MUSICAL COMEDY
the end

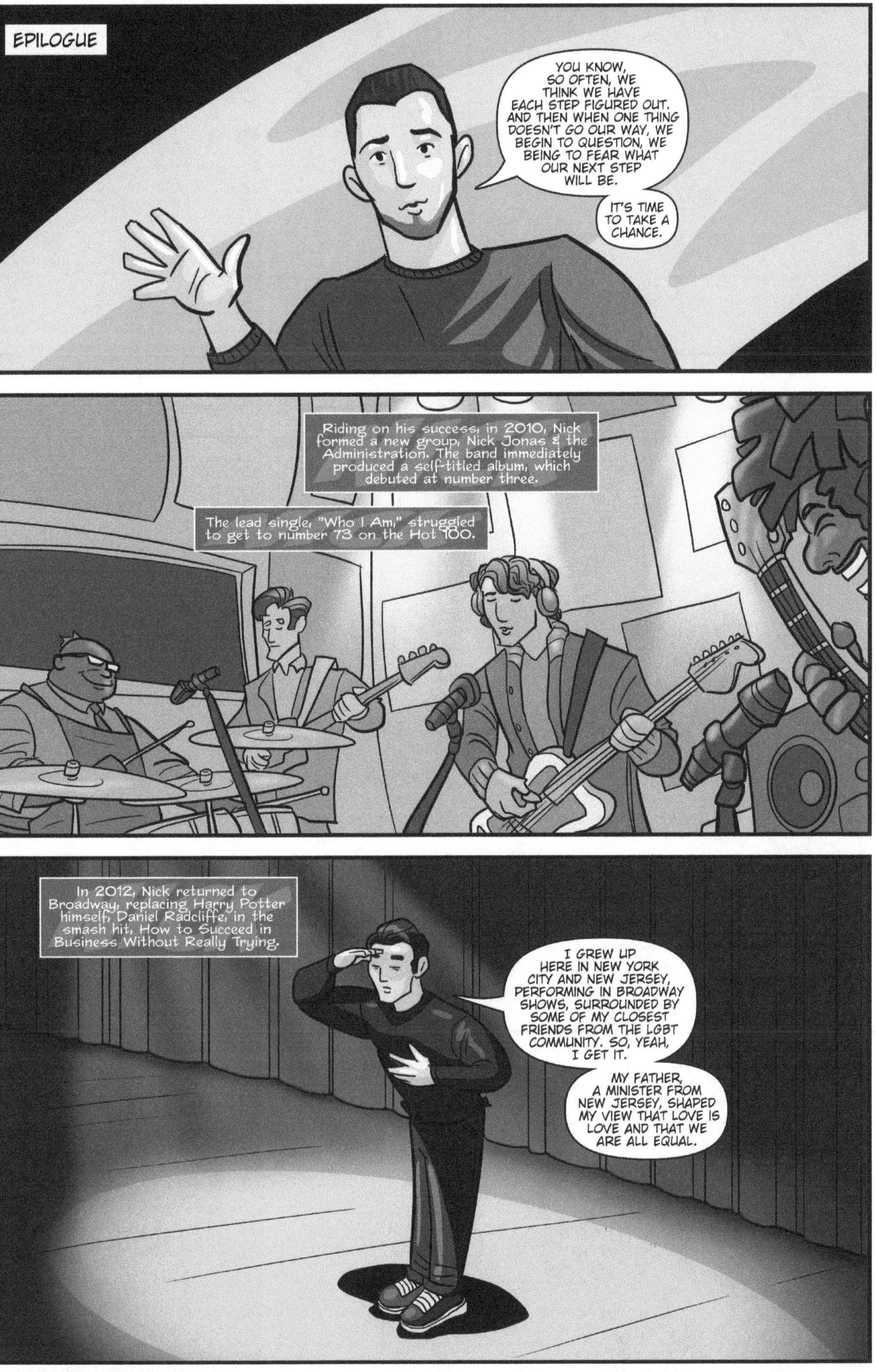
EPILOGUE
YOU KNOW, SO OFTEN, WE THINK WE HAVE EACH STEP FIGURED OUT. AND THEN WHEN ONE THING DOESN'T GO OUR WAY, WE BEGIN TO QUESTION, WE BEING TO FEAR WHAT OUR NEXT STEP WILL BE.
IT'S TIME TO TAKE A CHANCE.
Riding on his success, in 2010, Nick formed a new group, Nick Jonas & the Administration. The band immediately produced a self-titled album, which debuted at number three.
The lead single, "Who I Am," struggled to get to number 73 on the Hot 100.
In 2012, Nick returned to Broadway, replacing Harry Potter himself, Daniel Radcliffe, in the smash hit, How to Succeed in Business Without Really Trying.
I GREW UP HERE IN NEW YORK CITY AND NEW JERSEY, PERFORMING IN BROADWAY SHOWS, SURROUNDED BY SOME OF MY CLOSEST FRIENDS FROM THE LGBT COMMUNITY. SO, YEAH, I GET IT.
MY FATHER, A MINISTER FROM NEW JERSEY, SHAPED MY VIEW THAT LOVE IS LOVE AND THAT WE ARE ALL EQUAL.

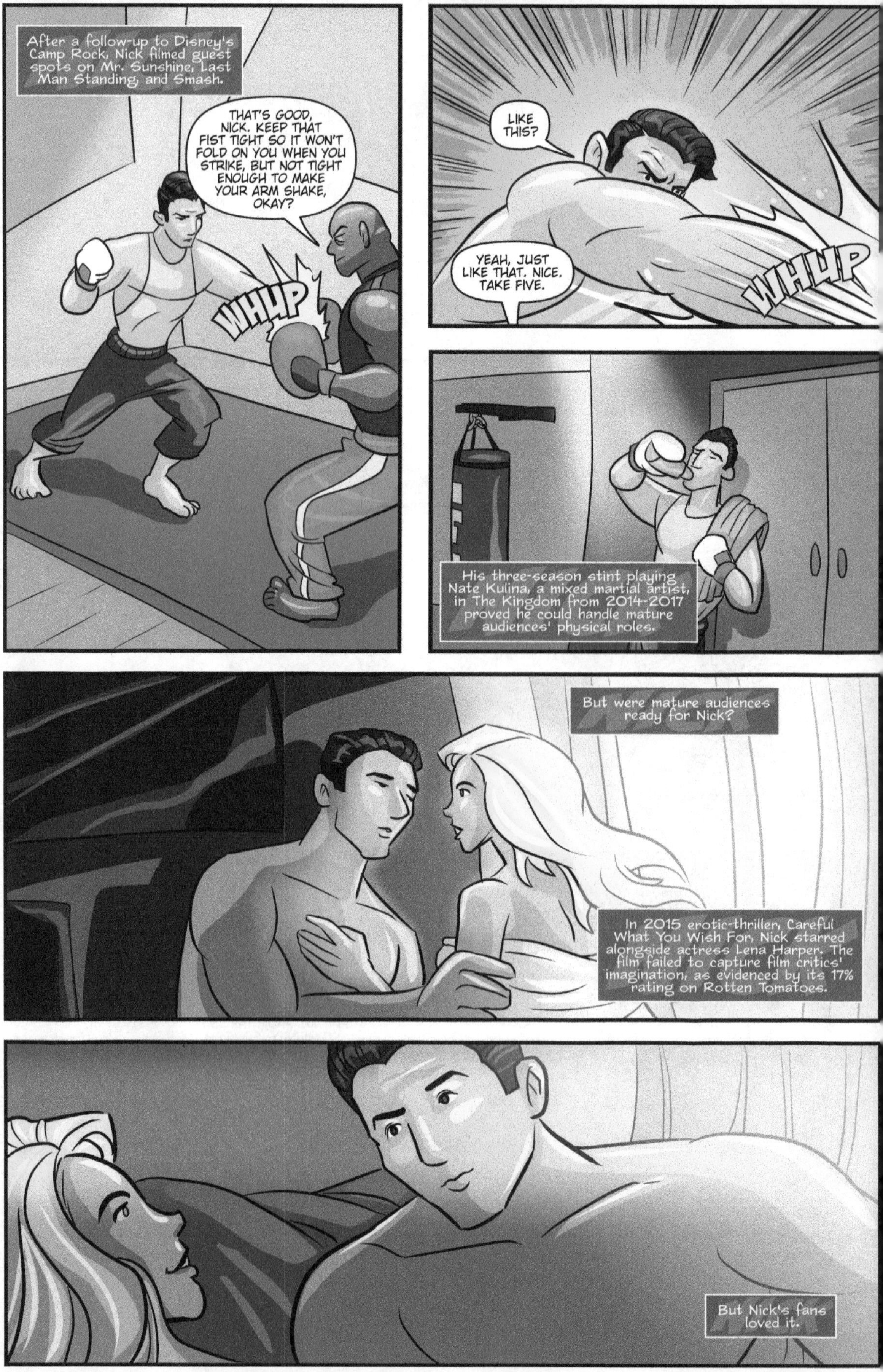
After a follow-up to Disney's Camp Rock, Nick filmed guest spots on Mr. Sunshine, Last Man Standing, and Smash.
THAT'S GOOD, NICK. KEEP THAT FIST TIGHT SO IT WON'T FOLD ON YOU WHEN YOU STRIKE, BUT NOT TIGHT ENOUGH TO MAKE YOUR ARM SHAKE, OKAY?
WHUP
LIKE THIS?
YEAH, JUST LIKE THAT. NICE. TAKE FIVE.
WHUP
His three-season stint playing Nate Kulina, a mixed martial artist, in The Kingdom from 2014-2017 proved he could handle mature audiences' physical roles.
But were mature audiences ready for Nick?
In 2015 erotic-thriller, Careful What You Wish For, Nick starred alongside actress Lena Harper. The film failed to capture film critics' imagination, as evidenced by its 17% rating on Rotten Tomatoes.
But Nick's fans loved it.

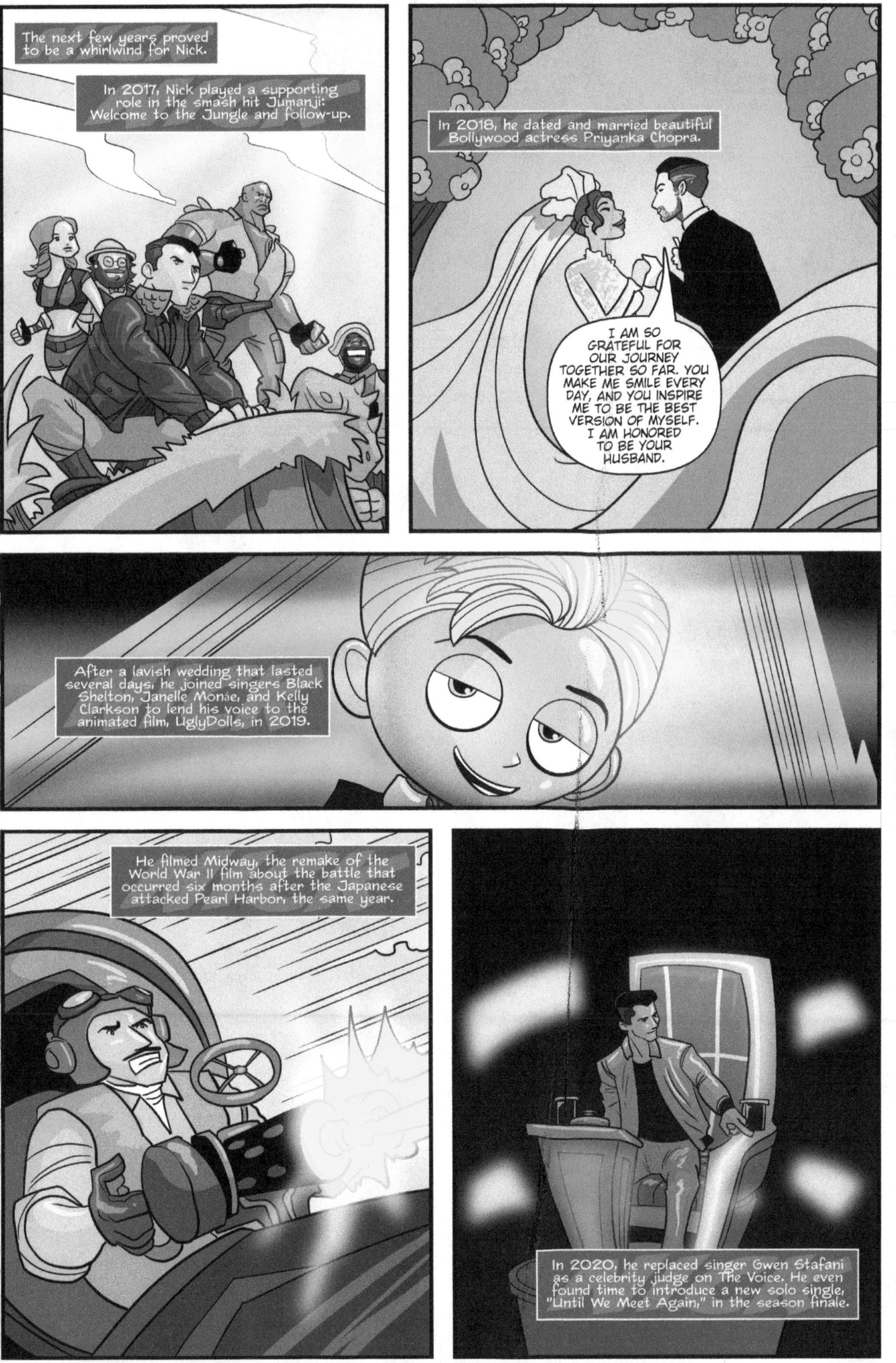

The next few years proved to be a whirlwind for Nick.
In 2017, Nick played a supporting role in the smash hit Jumanji: Welcome to the Jungle and follow-up.
In 2018, he dated and married beautiful Bollywood actress Priyanka Chopra.
I AM SO GRATEFUL FOR OUR JOURNEY TOGETHER SO FAR. YOU MAKE ME SMILE EVERY DAY, AND YOU INSPIRE ME TO BE THE BEST VERSION OF MYSELF. I AM HONORED TO BE YOUR HUSBAND.
After a lavish wedding that lasted several days, he joined singers Black Shelton, Janelle Monáe, and Kelly Clarkson to lend his voice to the animated film, UglyDolls, in 2019.
He filmed Midway, the remake of the World War II film about the battle that occurred six months after the Japanese attacked Pearl Harbor, the same year.
In 2020, he replaced singer Gwen Stafani as a celebrity judge on The Voice. He even found time to introduce a new solo single, "Until We Meet Again," in the season finale.

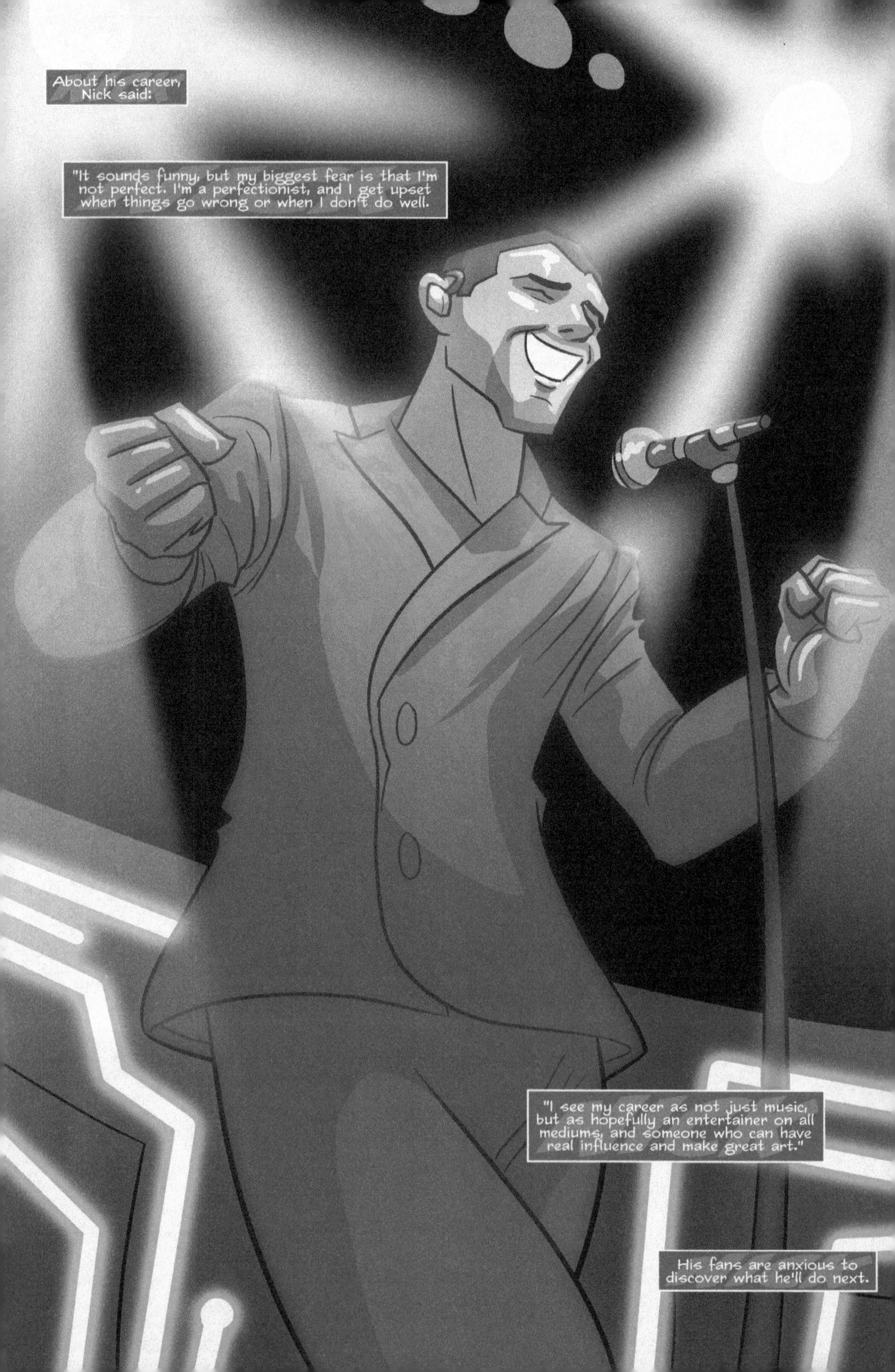
About his career, Nick said:
"It sounds funny, but my biggest fear is that I'm not perfect. I'm a perfectionist, and I get upset when things go wrong or when I don't do well.
"I see my career as not just music, but as hopefully an entertainer on all mediums, and someone who can have real influence and make great art."
His fans are anxious to discover what he'll do next.

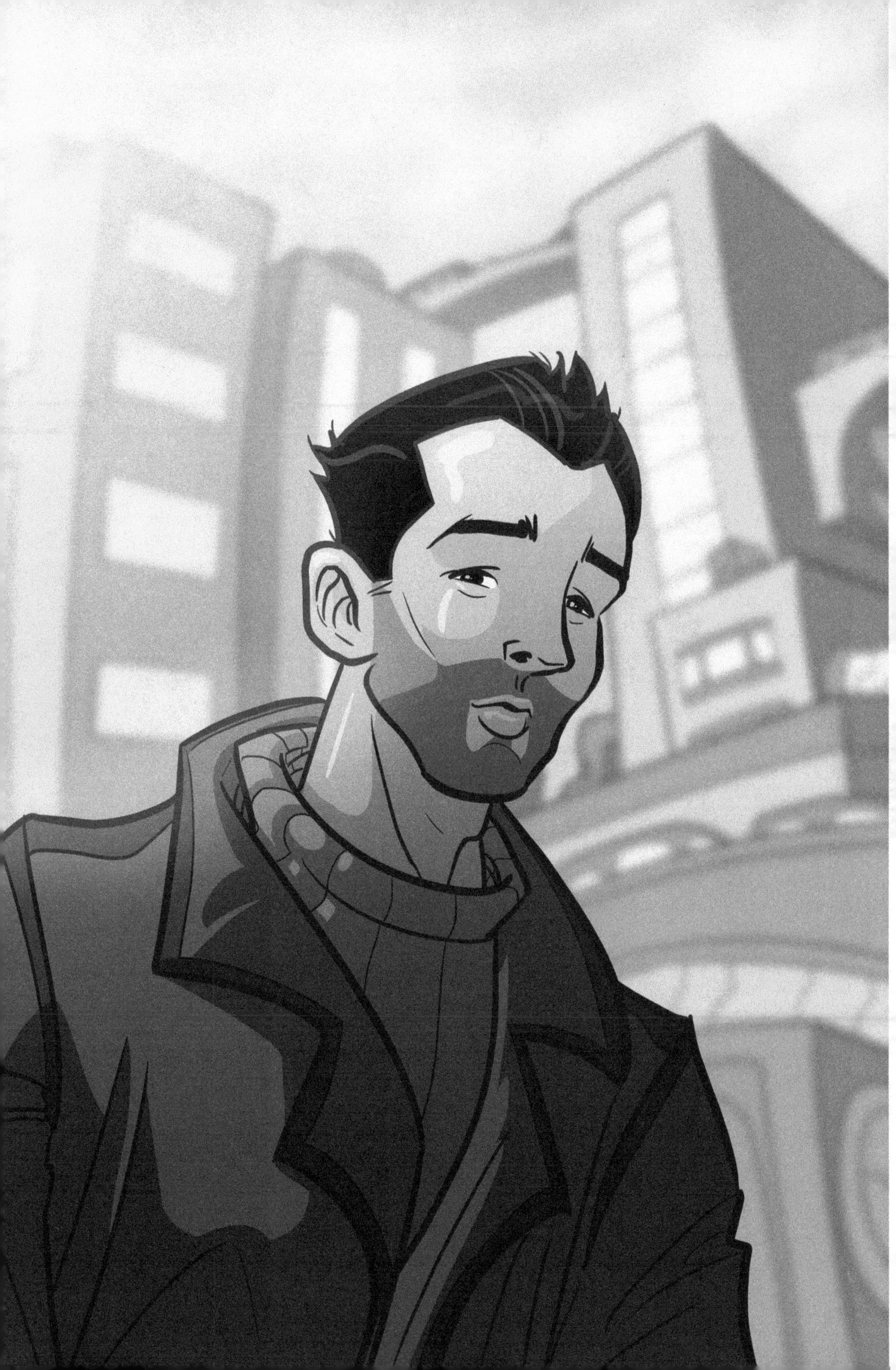

TIDALWAVE COMICS

Michael Frizell and Raphael Moran — Writer

Ramon Salas and Jill Lamarina — Pencils

Benjamin Glibert — Letters

Ramon Salas and Jill Lamarina — Colors

Ramon Salas — Cover

Darren G. Davis
Publisher

Maggie Jessup
Publicity

Susan Ferris
Entertainment Manager

TIDALWAVE PRODUCTIONS

CPSIA information can be obtained
at www.ICGtesting.com
Printed in the USA
BVHW061815130421
604817BV00008B/440

9 781954 044319